THIS BOOK

BELONGS TO

MEN'S RECORDS CROSSWORD

Across

3. Who is the shortest player to have been in the top 100 on the men's tour standing at 5'4" (163cm)? (6)

6. John Isner and which other player took part in the longest match in tennis history? (5)

8. Which player has won the calendar grand slam (winning all 4 majors in 1 year) twice in the 1960s? (5)

10. Which player holds the record for the most consecutive tour wins, who achieved this feat in 1978? (4)

11. Who is the tallest tennis player on the tour? (8)

12. Which unorthodox French player is third on the list for the most appearances in grand slams? (7)

14. Which American player holds the record for the most consecutive aces (10) being hit in a single match? (7)

17. Which player is the only men's player to be ranked number one in the world (1998) without winning a grand slam? (4)

18. Which Russian player broke 48 rackets in anger in a single season in 1999?

19. Rafael Nadal and which other player have won the most Davis cup titles?

20. Which player has won the most masters 1000 events?

Down

1. Who set the record for the fastest recorded serve of 162mph ever in 2012? (5)

2. Who holds the record for the greatest number of slams won by an American player? (7)

4. Which player holds the record for the most career singles titles? (7)

5. Which player hit a whopping 1466 aces in a single season in 1996, and still holds the record? (10)

7. Who has won the most Australian open titles? (7)

9. Who holds the record for the most Olympic singles titles? (6)

13. How many French open titles has Rafael Nadal won? (6)

15. To the nearest hour, how long was the longest match in tennis history? (6)

16. Roger Federer and which other player hold the record for losing in the most grand slam finals being 11? (5)

WIMBLEDON QUIZ

1. Which player won Wimbledon three years in a row between 1934-1936?

2. Who holds the record for the greatest number of Wimbledon titles in the ladies singles?

3. What type of bird is employed by Wimbledon to scare the other birds away, and is called Rufus?

4. To the nearest 2000, what is the capacity of Wimbledon centre court?

5. When did the first ever Wimbledon championships take place?

    a. 1845   b. 1866   c. 1877 d. 1885

6. What colour were the tennis balls at Wimbledon before 1986?

7. How old was Boris Becker when he first won Wimbledon in 1985?

8. Pete Sampras dominated the tournament in the 1990's, winning the tournament every year from 1993-2000 except for 1996. Who won it that year?

9. How many Wimbledon titles have the Williams sisters won between them?

10. What colour must all players wear at Wimbledon, but at no other tournaments?

11. Who won the Wimbledon ladies' singles title in 2019?

12. What was the score when Murray beat Djokovic in the 2013 Wimbledon final?

   a. 6-4 7-5 6-4   b. 6-4 3-6 7-6 6-2   c. 6-3 7-6 6-3

13. Who did Murray beat in 2016 to win his second Wimbledon title?

14. Which Belgian player (first name Steve) knocked Nadal out of Wimbledon in the first round in 2013?

15. How much prize money did the winners of Wimbledon receive in 2019?

   a. £1.75 mil   b. £1.85 mil   c. £2.05 mil   d. £2.25 mil

16. Which British tennis player, then ranked 772, made it through pre-qualifying and qualifying before losing to Federer in the second round of Wimbledon in 2016?

17. What year did Jamie Murray and Jelena Jankovic win the Mixed doubles at Wimbledon?

18. What was the score of the final set in the Isner Mahut epic match?

   a. 40-38   b. 50-48   c. 60-58   d. 70-68

19. How many singles titles has Federer won at Wimbledon?

20. How many tennis balls are used at Wimbledon every year?

   a. 40000 b. 45000   c. 54000   d. 65000

ROGER FEDERER CROSSWORD

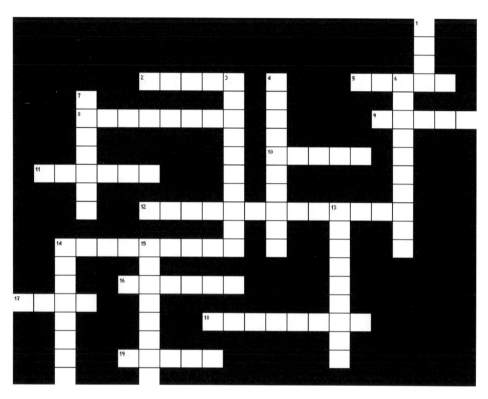

Across

2. What is Federer's wife called? (5)

5. In which Swiss city was Federer born in? (5)

8. At what sporting event did Federer meet his now wife? (8)

9. Which two tournaments has Federer won ten or more times? Basel and ….. (5)

10. Who did Federer beat in the final of his 20th grand slam win in 2018? (5)

11. After his sponsorship with Nike ended in 2018, which company did he sign up for as the replacement? (6)

12. Who did Federer beat in 2003 to win his first grand slam? (13)

14. What was Federer's first grand slam win in 2003? (9)

16. Who did Federer beat in the final of the 2008 US open? (6)

17. Between 2013 and 2016, how many grand slams did Federer win? (4)

18. Which player has beaten Federer the most (27 times)? (8)

19. Where did Federer win his first ever title in 2001? (5)

Down

1. How many times has Federer finished the year as world number one? (4)

3. Which grand slam did he win for his 20th career major? (10)

4. At which tournament did Federer complete his career grand slam in 2009? (6,4)

6. Who did Federer lose to in the second round of Wimbledon in 2013? (10)

7. Who did Federer beat 16-14 in the final of Wimbledon in 2009? (7)

13. Who did Federer beat in the final of the French open in 2009? (9)

14. Who did Federer win the Olympic gold with in doubles in 2008? (8)

15. Who has been Federer's main coach since 2016? (8)

THERE'S NO WAY AROUND HARD WORK. EMBRACE IT

-Roger Federer

TENNIS HISTORY QUIZ

1. When did the open era of tennis begin?

2. Which racket company introduced the first non-wooden racket?

    a. Wilson   b. Prince   c. Dunlop   d. Slazenger

3. Which of the four grand slams did Bjorn Borg win?

4. Which American tennis player holds the record for the most titles (singles and doubles) in men's tennis?

5. How many grand slam singles titles did Martina Navratilova win?

    a. 13   b. 14   c. 16   d. 18

6. Which female tennis player is the only person to have won the golden slam, meaning all four singles titles and the Olympic gold in the same year?

7. Which was the first grand slam to award equal prize money for men and women?

8. When were all masters 1000 events changed to best of three sets rather than best of five?

    a. 2004   b. 2006   c. 2008   d. 2010

9. How many consecutive Wimbledon titles did Bjorn Borg win?

10. How many grand slam singles titles did Martina Hingis win?

    a. 4   b. 5   c. 6   d. 7

11. When did Fred Perry win his last Wimbledon title?

12. What nationality is Roy Emerson who won 12 grand slam singles titles?

13. When was the last time that Wimbledon was cancelled other than 2020 due to coronavirus?

14. Which grand slam started the most recently?

15. How many grand slams did Boris Becker win?

    a. 5   b. 6   c. 7   d. 8

16. When was the fifth set tiebreaker at 12-12 introduced at Wimbledon?

17. Which two women are the only two in history to play each other in four consecutive grand slam finals?

18. Which country is believed to have invented tennis in the 12ᵗʰ century?

    a. Germany   b. France   c. Sweden   d. England

19. When was tennis added for the second time to the Olympic games?

    a. 1960   b. 1968   c. 1976   d. 1988

20. Which of these players has won more career matches?

    a. Roger Federer   b. Ken Rosewell   c. Jimmy Connors   d. Roy Emerson

SERENA WILLIAMS CROSSWORD

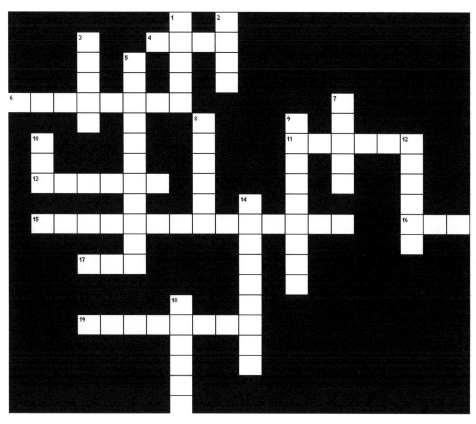

Across

4. Serena has lost in her last 4 grand slam finals. How many sets has she won in these? (4)

6. How many doubles grand slam titles has she won? (8)

11. Which young phenomenon did she beat to win her first grand slam? (6)

13. To the nearest $10 million how much prize money has Serena won in her career? (6)

15. Where did Serena win her most recent grand slam in 2017? (10,4)

16. In which country was Serena born? (3)

17. What is Serena's career high doubles ranking? (3)

19. Which animated TV show did Serena and Venus voice themselves in in 2001? (8)

Down

1. How many Wimbledon titles has Serena won? (5)

2. How many Olympic gold medals has Serena won (singles and doubles)? (4)

3. What round did Murray and Serena lose in in the 2019 mixed doubles at Wimbledon? (5)

5. How many grand slam singles titles has Serena won? (6,5)

7. In 2015 Serena was on the verge of a career grand slam until she lost in the semi-final to which Italian player? (5)

8. Who has Serena won her two mixed doubles grand slam titles with? (6)

9. Which 17-year-old beat Serena in the final of Wimbledon in 2004? (9)

10. How many grand slam finals has Serena lost? (3)

12. Which player stunned Serena with a straight sets win in the US open final in 2011? (6)

14. Which young Canadian woman beat Serena in the 2019 US open? (9)

18. Where did a 17-year-old Serena win her first grand slam title in 1999? (2,4)

LUCK HAS NOTHING TO DO WITH IT

-Serena Williams

TENNIS RULES QUIZ

1. Where is a vibration dampener usually placed on a tennis racket?

2. If a player's racket touches the net, then what is the umpire's correct call?

3. Yes or no? A player can jump over the net mid-point if they do not touch the net.

4. What happens when a ball from another match comes onto the court mid-point?

5. In doubles, what happens if the receiving player at the net is hit by the serve?

    a. A let is played   b. The receiver wins the point   c. The server wins the point

6. A player hits a ball that strikes the singles stick and goes in mid-point. Is the ball in play?

    a. Yes   b. No   c. Yes, but not if it was a serve

7. How many bounces are allowed in wheelchair tennis?

8. If the ball bounces twice just before the player hits it, what does the umpire say?

9. What is the official length of a warm-up prior to the start of a match?

10. After winning a coin toss the player has four options. The first three are to either serve, to receive, or to choose what end you want, but what is the fourth option?

    a. To serve from a particular end   b. To receive from a particular end   c. Ask the opponent to make the choice

11. What is different about changing ends at 1-0 in a set compared to all the others changes of ends?

12. At 3-2 in the first set when changing ends, how long are the players allowed to rest before resuming play?

    a.   60 seconds at their chair but they must be playing within a further 30 seconds after that

    b.   90 seconds at their chair but they must be playing immediately after that

    c.   90 seconds at their chair but they must be playing within a further 30 seconds after that

13. When are toilet breaks allowed in a tennis match?

14. How long is a super tiebreak, also known as a match tiebreak?

15. How often do players change sides in a tiebreak?

16. Is the receiver allowed to return the serve before it has bounced?

17. If a player is quick enough, are they allowed to volley the ball before it has crossed the net onto their side?

18. After a tiebreak, who serves first in the next set?

    a. The player that served the 1st point in the previous set tiebreak

    b. The player that received the 1st point in the previous set tiebreak

    c. The winner of the previous set tiebreak

    d. The loser of the previous set tiebreak

19. What happens if the server throws the ball up, and swings but completely misses the ball?

20. In professional tennis, players are not allowed to serve underarm. True or false?

WOMEN'S RECORDS CROSSWORD

Across

5. Which Belgian player is the only woman since 1996 to reach all four grand slam finals in the same year? (5)

7. Who is the most recent player to win a slam after having a baby? (9)

8. Steffi Graf holds the record for the most consecutive grand slam finals, but how many was it? (8)

10. Which tennis legend recently had a film made about her called battle of the sexes? (4)

11. Which Italian player who has won one grand slam is fourth on the list for all time slam appearances? (9)

13. Which American tennis player is the tallest player to ever win a grand slam singles event? (9)

15. Which Russian player is the most recent to reach all four grand slam finals in their career in 2012? (9)

16. Which grand slam champion did Schiavone beat 16-14 in the third set at the Australian Open to win the longest grand slam match ever? (10)

18. Who is second on the list for all time grand slams won in the open era? (4)

Down

1. Which British female tennis player has won the most titles since 2000? (6)

2. How old was Jennifer Capriati when she set the record to be the youngest player to reach the top ten? (8)

3. Who is Great Britain's most recent woman to have won a grand slam? (4)

4. Connolly, Court and Navratilova hold the record for the most consecutive grand slam titles, but how long was this streak? (3)

5. Which Swiss player spent 209 weeks as world number one, making her fifth on the list? (6)

6. Which Slovakian player is the shortest player to ever reach a grand slam final in 2014? (9)

9. Which player has won the most overall titles? (11)

11. By their first name, who holds the record for the most match wins at the Australian Open? (6)

12. Which American player has made the most grand slam appearances with 84? (8)

14. Who holds the record for the most grand slam titles, with 13 coming before the open era, and 11 coming after? (5)

17. Which player born in 1954 holds the record for the most singles grand slam finals with 34? (5)

ANDY MURRAY QUIZ

1. Which Scottish city was Andy Murray born in?

   a. Edinburgh   b. Glasgow   c. Aberdeen

2. At what age did Murray start playing tennis?

   a. 8   b. 10   c. 5   d. 3

3. Which of these tennis greats has been Murray's coach?

   a. McEnroe   b. Lendl   c. Borg   d. Becker

4. What year did Murray win his first slam?

5. Which of the four grand slams did Murray win first?

6. Who did Murray beat in the final of his first Wimbledon win?

7. Murray's first grand slam appearance saw him reach the last 32 at Wimbledon in 2005, but who beat him?

8. Where did Murray win his first title in 2006?

   a. San Jose   b. San Francisco   c. San Diego   d. St Petersburg

9. In 2012 Murray won Olympic gold, but who did he beat in the semi final and final to do so?

   a. Del Potro & Djokovic   b. Nadal & Federer   c. Djokovic & Federer

10. How many times has Murray been runner-up at the Australian Open?

11. Murray guided Great Britain to their first Davis Cup win since 1936 in 2015. Which team did Great Britain beat in the final?

12. Who did Murray beat to win his second Olympic gold in Rio in 2016?

13. How many consecutive wins did Murray get at the end of the 2016 season?

   a. 21   b. 23   c. 24   d. 27

14. How many titles did Murray win in 2016?

   a. 8   b. 9   c. 10   d. 11

15. How many times has Murray reached the French Open final?

16. Which member of the 'big three' has Murray beaten the fewest times?

17. How many times has Murray won Queens?

   a. 5   b. 6   c. 7   d. 8

18. Who was his partner when won he won the doubles at Queens in 2019?

19. Who did Murray beat in the final at the European Open in Antwerp in 2019?

20. How many coaches has Murray worked with throughout his career?

   a. 5   b. 7   c. 8   d. 10

I CAN CRY LIKE ROGER.
IT'S JUST A SHAME I
CAN'T PLAY LIKE HIM

-Andy Murray

MARIA SHARAPOVA CROSSWORD

Across

1. What family member coached Sharapova for most of her career? (6)

3. Where is Sharapova from? (6)

6. To the nearest 10 million, how much prize money did Sharapova win during her career? (5)

7. Where did Sharapova finish in the 2012 Olympics? (6)

9. Which famous tennis player did Sharapova date in 2013? (8)

12. Which famous tennis academy did Sharapova train at when she was a kid? (11)

14. Which player with a single hander did Sharapova beat in the final of the 2006 US Open to win her second major title? (5)

16. What is Sharapova's candy and chocolate line called? (9)

17. How many majors did Sharapova win in total? (4)

18. How old was Sharapova when she made her professional debut, losing to Monica Seles? (8)

Down

2. Which Italian player did Sharapova beat in the final of the French Open in 2012 to complete her career grand slam? (6)

4. What country does Sharapova live in as of 2020? (7)

5. In which capital city did Sharapova win her first title in 2003? (5)

8. Where did Sharapova win her first grand slam title as a 17-year-old? (9)

10. In inches, how much taller than 6 foot is Sharapova? (3)

11. Where did Sharapova win her final major? (6,4)

13. Which Serbian player did Sharapova beat in the final of the 2008 Australian Open to win her third major title? (8)

15. Which company sponsored Sharapova? (4)

17

I WANT MY TENNIS
TO SPEAK
FOR EVERYTHING
-Maria Sharapova

GRAND SLAM WINNERS QUIZ

1. Which Swedish man won the Australian Open in 2002?

2. Which Japanese woman won the US Open in 2018?

3. How many grand slams did Marat Safin win?

4. Which Spanish woman won the French Open in 2016?

5. Which Argentinian man won the French Open in 2004?

6. How many grand slams did Marion Bartoli win?

7. Which Brazilian player won the French open three times in 1997, 2000 and 2001?

8. How many grand slams did Lleyton Hewitt win?

9. Which Australian women won the US Open in 2011?

10. Which American woman won the Australian Open in 2020?

11. Which Australian man won the US Open in 1997 and 1998?

12. In what year did Caroline Wozniaki win the Australian Open?

13. How many grand slams did Victoria Azarenka win?

14. How many grand slams did Andre Agassi win?

15. Which male player won the French Open in 1998 whose first name is Carlos?

16. When did Ostapenko win the French Open?

17. How many grand slams did Pete Sampras win?

18. What was the first grand slam that Li Na won in 2011?

19. What nationality was eight-time grand slam champion Ivan Lendl?

20. In what year did Bianca Andreescu win the US Open?

RAFAEL NADAL CROSSWORD

Across

3. How many French Open titles has Nadal won? (6)

5. Which Chilean player did Nadal beat in the final of the 2008 Rio Olympics? (8)

6. Which retired Russian player has a 6-5 winning record against Nadal? (9)

8. How many Wimbledon titles has Nadal won? (3)

10. Who did Nadal beat in the final of the US Open in 2019 to win his 19th slam title? (8)

12. What masters 1000 event has Nadal reached the final of five times without winning it? (5)

13. Who beat Nadal in the French Open in 2009 in the fourth round? (9)

14. What is the first name of Nadal's uncle and coach? (4)

16. Which Spanish former player joined Nadal's coaching team in 2016? (4)

17. What country is Nadal from? (5)

18. How many times has Nadal beaten Federer in the French Open final? (4)

Down

1. How many Wimbledon finals has Nadal played in? (4)

2. How many end of year season finals has Nadal won? (2)

4. Nadal became the second player to win the French Open on their first attempt. Which Swedish player was the first? (8)

5. Which Spanish player did Nadal retire against in the French Open in 2016? (10)

7. As a 17-year-old, who did Nadal beat in the final of the French Open for his first slam title? His first name is Mariano (6)

9. For which artist did Nadal appear in a music video for in 2010? (7)

11. Who beat Nadal in the quarter finals of the French Open in 2015? (8)

12. What is the first name of Nadal's wife? (5)

15. How many US Opens has Nadal won? (4)

LOSING IS NOT MY ENEMY...
FEAR OF LOSING
IS MY ENEMY

-Rafael Nadal

GUESS THE PLAYER QUIZ

1. This French male tennis player was born in 1986 and achieved a career high ranking of world number 6 in 2016. He is famous for his jump smash and all-round flair.

2. This Australian female tennis player was once a professional cricket player. She was born in 1996 and has won 8 singles titles.

3. This Greek male tennis player was born in 1998 and has achieved a career high ranking of world number 5.

4. This Canadian female tennis player is 26 years old and reached the Wimbledon final in 2014.

5. This Russian female tennis player was born in 1985, and appeared in 4 grand slam finals, winning two of them.

6. This Canadian male tennis player was born in 1990 and achieved a career high ranking of world number 3.

7. This Serbian male tennis player was born in 1986 and achieved a career high ranking of world number 12 in 2011. He served a one-year doping ban in 2013-14 for missing a drugs test.

8. This French female tennis player was born in 1993 and has a career high singles ranking of number 10, and a career high doubles ranking of number 1. She was dating tennis star Dominic Thiem in 2019.

9. This is a Belgian male tennis player who was born in 1990. He made the end of year tour finals in 2017 and made the Wimbledon quarter finals in 2019.

10. This is a Russian male tennis player, who was born in 1997. As of 2020 he has won four singles titles and has a career high ranking of 14.

11. This Puerto Rican female tennis player was born in 1993. She has a career high world ranking of 27 and stunned everyone by winning gold at the 2016 Rio Olympics.

12. This Georgian male tennis player was born in 1992. He reached a career high ranking of 16 in 2019 and is a two-time winner of the German Open.

13. This Czech player has won 16 singles and five doubles titles on the WTA tour. She reached her only grand slam final at the US Open in 2016 where she lost to Kerber in three sets.

14. This Croatian male tennis player was born in 1996. He reached a career high singles ranking of 12 in 2018 and has made the fourth round at both Wimbledon and the Australian Open.

15. This is a Swiss female tennis player who was born in 1997. She achieved her highest ranking of number 4 in the world at the start of 2020, and her first and second name both begin with the same letter.

16. This player famously got disqualified after hitting the umpire in the face with a tennis ball while he was losing against Murray in the Davis Cup.

17. This female player was born in 1998 and is the youngest American player to win a slam since Serena Williams in 2002.

18. This male player was born in 1985. He has won 18 singles titles and made the final of the Australian Open in 2008. Later in his career he started switching from a double hander to a single hander.

19. This female tennis player is married to famous German footballer Schweinsteiger. She is the former world number one and won the French Open in 2008.

20. This Argentinian male tennis player turned pro in 2010. He is the shortest male tennis player to reach a grand slam quarter final since 1994, standing at 1.70m (5 foot 7 inches)

GUESS THE TOURNAMENT CROSSWORD

Across

2. Which masters is held at Hard Rock Stadium, and was won by Roger Federer in 2019? (5)

4. Sponsored by Rolex, which masters was won in 2019 by Fabio Fognini? (5,5)

8. What city was the Rogers Cup played in in 2019 that was won by Nadal? (7)

9. Which is the first masters 1000 event of the year? (6,5)

14. Which tournament recently changed its name to the Fever-Tree championships? (6)

16. Where is the Nature Valley tournament played at (it is a Wimbledon warm up event)? (10)

17. At which tournament is the centre court called Stade Roland Garros? (6,4)

18. In which city were the 2019 Nitto ATP finals held? (6)

Down

1. What Wimbledon warm up event has a centre court called the Gerry Weber Stadion? (5)

3. In which city is China's only masters 1000 event? (8)

5. At which tournament is the centre court called the Rod Laver Arena? (10,4)

6. Which masters is known as the Western and Southern Open, and was won by Medvedev in 2019? (10)

7. In which city is the Internationale BNL d'Italia held? (4)

10. Which tournament is the oldest tournament in the world? (9)

11. In which European city were the Next Gen finals held in 2019? (5)

12. What is the final masters 1000 event of the year? (5)

13. Which masters runs at the start of May, and was won by Djokovic in 2019? (6)

15. At which tournament is the centre court called the Arthur Ashe Stadium, and is the largest of all tennis stadiums? (2,4

BRITISH TENNIS QUIZ

1. As of July 2020, what is Dan Evans' highest tennis ranking?

   a. 28   b. 22   c. 38   d. 18

2. Who did Heather Watson win the 2016 Wimbledon mixed doubles championship with?

3. At which grand slam did Kyle Edmund make the semi-finals in 2018?

4. What was Johanna Konta's highest career ranking back in 2017?

5. What is the name of the British male tennis player who is ranked 77 in the world (as of July 2020), and graduated from Texas University in 2017.

6. What is Dan Evans' furthest run in a grand slam?

7. In what country was Johanna Konta born?

8. What tennis legend did Jamie Murray win the mixed doubles with at Wimbledon and the US open in 2017?

9. How many times did Tim Henman make the Wimbledon semi-final?

10. At which grand slam did Greg Rusedski reach the final in 1997?

11. Which is the only grand slam that Virginia Wade did not win?

12. What was Tim Henman's career high ranking?

13. Who did Heather Watson famously lose to in the third round of Wimbledon in 2015?

14. How many career titles has Johanna Konta won?

   a. 3   b. 4   c. 5   d. 6

15. How many career titles has Kyle Edmund won?

   a. 0   b. 1   c. 2   d. 3

16. Heather Watson won her first title at the Japan Open in 2012. How many years had it been since a British female player had won a title before that?

   a. 6 years   b. 12 years   c. 18 years   d. 24 years

17. Who did Marcus Willis play with, beating the defending Wimbledon doubles champions Mahut and Herbert in 2017?

18. Which British female made the finals of the junior Australian Open in 2015?

19. In what year was Joanna Konta born?

   a. 1987   b. 1989   c. 1991   d. 1993

20. In which country was Kyle Edmund born?

   a. Argentina   b. Belgium   c. Australia   d. South Africa

NOVAK DJOKOVIC CROSSWORD

Across

1. Who did Djokovic beat in the final of the French Open in 2016 to win his only title there? (6)

5. What small country does Djokovic live in as of 2020? (6)

8. How many times has Djokovic ended the year as world number one? (4)

10. Djokovic went on a 14 grand slam run in which he at least made it to the semis. Who broke his run at the 2014 Australian Open? (8)

12. How many grand slam titles has Djokovic won? (9)

13. Who did Djokovic beat to win his first ever end of year world tour finals? (9)

14. Which former grand slam winner did Djokovic lose to at his first grand slam tournament in 2005? (5)

15. Which Croatian former tennis player is one of Djokovic's current coaches? (10)

17. In 2011 Djokovic won the Australian Open final by losing just 9 games. Who was his opponent? (6)

18. Who did he beat at the 2008 Australian Open to win his first major title? (6)

Down

2. Where did he reach his first major final in 2007? (2,4)

3. How many times has Djokovic won the season ending finals? (4)

4. Who did Djokovic lose to in his first slam final in 2007? (7)

6. In 2018 he completed his career golden masters (winning every masters 1000 event). At which event did he finish this feat? (10)

7. In 2011 Djokovic got off to an amazing start, not losing a match until the French Open. How many matches did he win in a row? (5,3)

9. Which Slovakian former tennis player is the other of Djokovic's current coaches? (5)

11. What is the first name of Djokovic's wife? (6)

16. What country is Djokovic from? (6)

THE WINNER IS THE ONE WHO BELIEVES IN VICTORY MORE

-Novak Djokovic

OLDEST AND YOUNGEST

1. Who was the youngest man to win Wimbledon?

2. How old was Federer when he won the Australian Open in 2018, becoming the oldest male player to win a slam since 1972?

3. Which 16-year-old winner of the Australian Open in 1997 is the youngest player ever to win a grand slam?

4. Who was the youngest ever male grand slam winner?

5. Who is the oldest tennis player currently playing on the tennis tour as of July 2020?

6. Which then Yugoslavian female player was the youngest to win the French Open in 1990?

7. How old was Hingis when she won her first junior grand slam title?

8. Who is the oldest woman to win a grand slam?

9. Who is the youngest woman to win Wimbledon?

10. In what year were doubles legends Bob and Mike Bryan born? They have announced their retirement at the end of 2020.

    a. 1976   b. 1978   c. 1980   d. 1982

11. Who is the youngest male tennis player to be ranked world number one? This player achieved this in 2001

12. Who is the youngest female player to qualify for the main draw of Wimbledon, which she achieved in 2019?

13. How old was Hingis when she became the youngest player ever to be ranked world number one?

14. Which American became the youngest man to win the US Open at just 19 years old?

15. Federer recently set the record as the oldest world number one ever. How old was he?

ANSWERS

MEN'S RECORDS

WIMBLEDON QUIZ

1. Fred Perry

2. Martina Navratilova

3. Hawk

4. 15000

5. 1877

6. White

7. 17

8. Richard Krajicek

9. 12

10. White

11. Simona Halep

12. 6-4 7-5 6-4

13. Milos Raonic

14. Steve Darcis

15. £2.25 mil

16. Marcus Willis

17. 2007

18. 70-68

19. 8

20. 54000

FEDERER CROSSWORD

TENNIS HISTORY QUIZ

1. 1968

2. Wilson

3. French Open and Wimbledon

4. John McEnroe

5. 18

6. Steffi Graf

7. US Open

8. 2008

9. 5

10. 5

11. 1936

12. Australian

13. 1939-1945 due to the second world war

14. Australian Open

15. 6

16. 2019

17. Venus and Serena

18. France

19. 1988

20. Ken Rosewell

SERENA WILLIAMS CROSSWORD

TENNIS RULES QUIZ

1. Bottom centre of the racket

2. The player who touched the net loses the point

3. No

4. A let is played

5. The server wins the point

6. Yes, but not if it was a serve

7. Two

8. Not up

9. 5 minutes

10. Ask the opponent to make the choice

11. You are not allowed to sit down

12. 60 seconds at their chair but they must be playing within a further 30 seconds after that.

13. At the end of the set

14. 10 points

15. Every 6 points

16. No

17. No

18. The player that received the 1st point in the previous set tiebreak

19. It is a fault

20. False

WOMEN'S TENNIS RECORDS

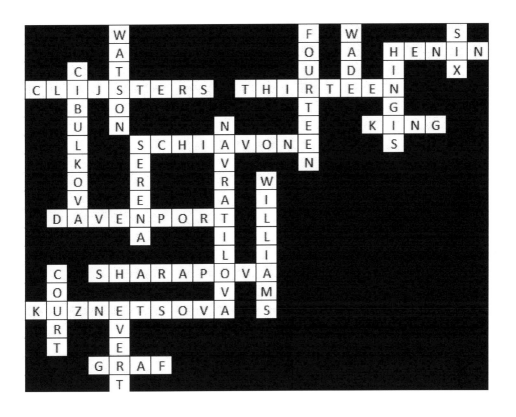

ANDY MURRAY QUIZ

1. Glasgow

2. 3

3. Lendl

4. 2012

5. US Open

6. Novak Djokovic

7. David Nalbandian

8. San Jose

9. Djokovic & Federer

10. Five times

11. Belgium

12. Juan Martin Del Potro

13. 24

14. 9

15. Once

16. Nadal

17. 5

18. Feliciano Lopez

19. Stan Wawrinka

20. 10

SHARAPOVA CROSSWORD

GRAND SLAM WINNERS QUIZ

1. Thomas Johansson

2. Naomi Osaka

3. Two

4. Garbine Muguruza

5. Gaston Gaudio

6. one

7. Gustavo Kuerten

8. two

9. Sam Stosur

10. Sofia Kenin

11. Patrick Rafter

12. 2018

13. two

14. eight

15. Carlos Moya

16. 2017

17. 14

18. French Open

19. Czech Republic

20. 2019

RAFAEL NADAL CROSSWORD

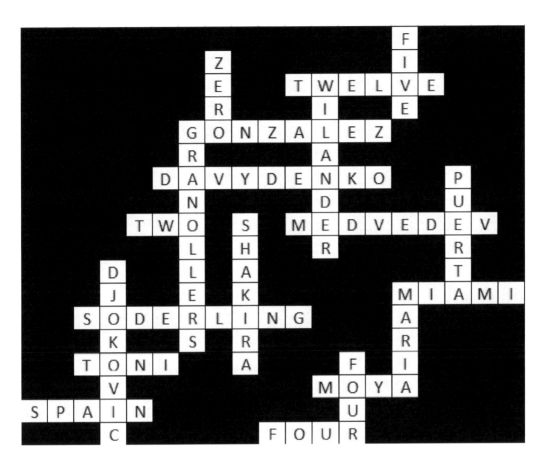

GUESS THE PLAYER

1. Gael Monfils

2. Ashleigh Barty

3. Stefanos Tsitsipas

4. Genie Bouchard

5. Svetlana Kuznetsova

6. Milos Raonic

7. Viktor Troicki

8. Kristina Mladenovic

9. David Goffin

10. Andrey Rublev

11. Monica Puig

12. Nikoloz Basilashvili

13. Karolína Plíšková

14. Borna Ćorić

15. Belinda Bencic

16. Denis Shapovalov

17. Sofia Kenin

18. Jo-Wilfried Tsonga

19. Ana Ivanović

20. Diego Schwartzman

GUESS THE TOURNAMENT CROSSWORD

BRITISH TENNIS QUIZ

1. 28

2. Henri Kontinen

3. Australian Open

4. 4

5. Cameron Norrie

6. Fourth round

7. Australia

8. Martina Hingis

9. 4

10. US Open

11. French Open

12. 4

13. Serena Williams

14. 3

15. 2

16. 24 years

17. Jay Clarke

18. Katie Swan

19. 1991

20. South Africa

DJOKOVIC CROSSWORD

OLDEST AND YOUNGEST QUIZ

1. Boris Becker

2. 36 years old

3. Martina Hingis

4. Michael Chang

5. Ivo Karlovic

6. Monica Seles

7. 12

8. Serena Williams

9. Maria Sharapova

10. 1978

11. Lleyton Hewitt

12. Coco Gauff

13. 16

14. Pete Sampras

15. 36

Printed in Great Britain
by Amazon